SOMERSET AND AVON RAILWAYS IN OLD PHOTOGRAPHS

SOMERSET AND AVON RAILWAYS IN OLD PHOTOGRAPHS

COLLECTED BY
KEVIN ROBERTSON

ALAN SUTTON

Alan Sutton Publishing Limited
Phoenix Mill · Far Thrupp · Stroud · Gloucestershire

First Published 1990

British Library Cataloguing in Publication Data

Somerset and Avon Railways in old photographs.
1. South-West England. Railway services, history
I. Robertson, Kevin
385.09423

ISBN 0–86299-800–X

Typeset in 9/10 Korinna.
Typesetting and origination by
Alan Sutton Publishing Limited.
Printed in Great Britain by
Dotesios Printers Limited.

CONTENTS

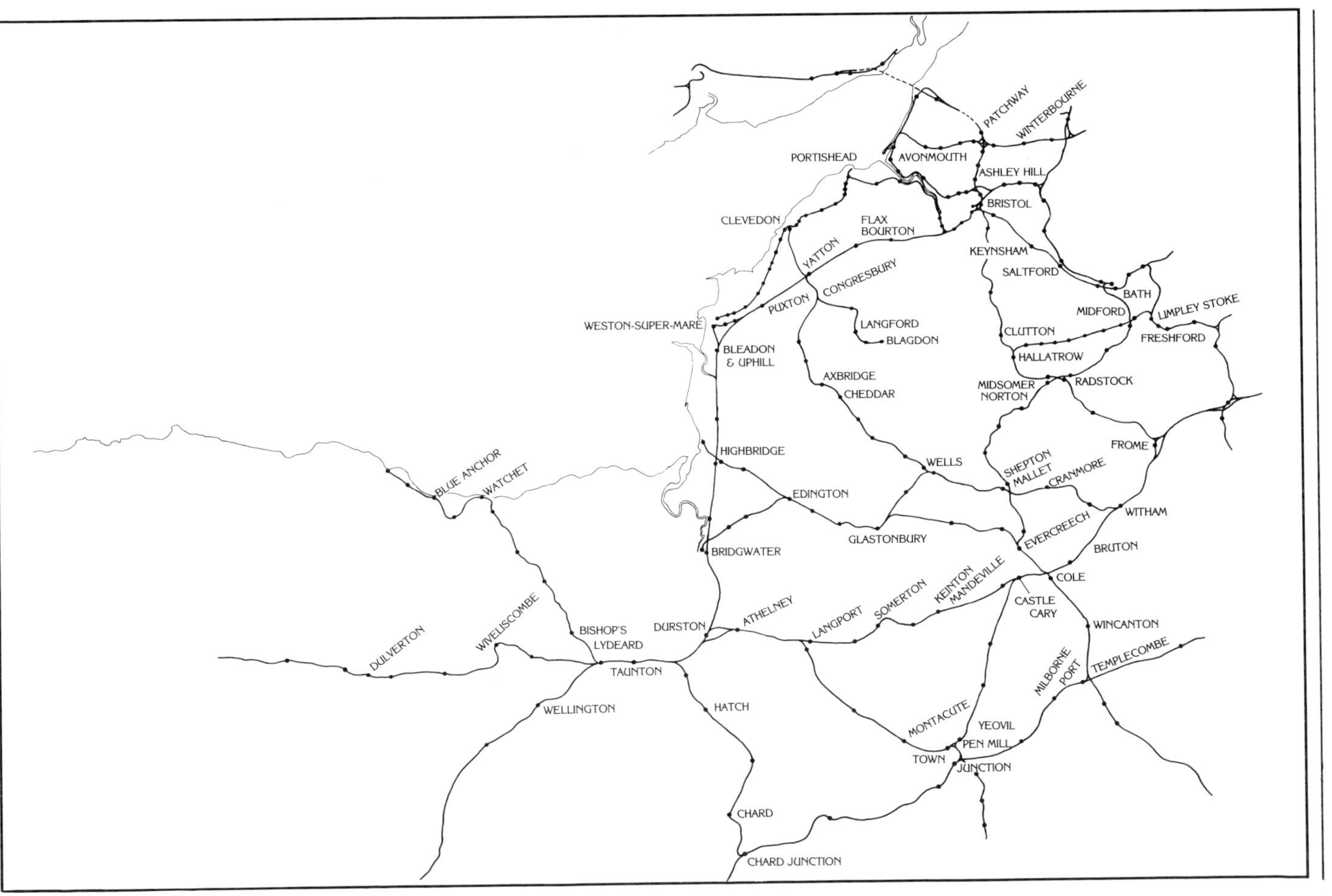
PATCHWAY
WINTERBOURNE
PORTISHEAD
AVONMOUTH
ASHLEY HILL
BRISTOL
CLEVEDON
FLAX BOURTON
KEYNSHAM
YATTON
SALTFORD
CONGRESBURY
BATH
PUXTON
MIDFORD
LIMPLEY STOKE
LANGFORD
WESTON-SUPER-MARE
BLAGDON
CLUTTON
FRESHFORD
BLEADON & UPHILL
HALLATROW
AXBRIDGE
CHEDDAR
MIDSOMER NORTON
RADSTOCK
FROME
HIGHBRIDGE
WELLS
SHEPTON MALLET
CRANMORE
BLUE ANCHOR
WATCHET
EDINGTON
WITHAM
GLASTONBURY
EVERCREECH
BRIDGWATER
BRUTON
KEINTON MANDEVILLE
COLE
SOMERTON
CASTLE CARY
ATHELNEY
LANGPORT
WINCANTON
DURSTON
BISHOP'S LYDEARD
WIVELISCOMBE
DULVERTON
TEMPLECOMBE
MILBORNE PORT
TAUNTON
WELLINGTON
HATCH
MONTACUTE
YEOVIL
PEN MILL
TOWN
JUNCTION
CHARD
CHARD JUNCTION

INTRODUCTION

In terms of history the county of Somerset is usually associated with Arthurian legend and the country of Avalon. Over the centuries fact and fiction have become interwoven into myth.

Somerset also lays claim, however, to having once been a thriving mining region and it was to service the needs of this industry that improvements to the transport system of the county were first contemplated. Enter, then, the various waterways such as the Somerset Coal Canal. As is well known, though, the age of the canal was destined to be short lived, superseded by the iron wheel and steel rail – the railway age.

The rapid nineteenth-century development of the main line railway network led to a vast number of through and branch line routes, many of these owing their origin to coal and aggregate extraction. Locations like Radstock and Frome owe their very development to mineral wealth and, while coal may no longer be extracted, stone continues to be an important export from the Mendip area.

In presenting this collection of old photographs, I am conscious that in a volume of restricted size it is not possible to cover every station and location. Instead I have concentrated on some of the least-known localities and included a section on the Somerset and Dorset from around the turn of the century with photographs which I know have not been seen before.

May I take this opportunity to thank Dennis Tillman for the plan, Lyn as ever for her tolerance and Colin Banks for his support.

Kevin Robertson.
Eastleigh 1990

OPENING OF LINES IN DATE ORDER.

Weston Super Mare branch	14.6.1841
London to Bristol	30.6.1841
Bristol to Exeter	1.5.1844
Bristol to Gloucester	17.6.1844
Clevedon Branch	28.7.1847
Westbury to Frome	7.10.1850
Durston to Yeovil	1.10.1853
Highbridge to Glastonbury	28.8.1854
Frome to Radstock	14.10.1854
Frome to Yeovil	1.9.1856
Yeovil to Weymouth	20.1.1857
Bathampton to Bradford-on-Avon	2.2.1857
Frome to Shepton Mallet	9.11.1858
Salisbury to Yeovil	1.6.1860
Yeovil to Exeter	19.7.1860
Somerset Central Railway	3.2.1862
Shepton Mallet to Wells	1.3.1862
Norton Fitzwarren to Watchet	31.3.1862
Chard Branch (LSWR)	8.5.1863
Bristol to New Passage	8.9.1863
Somerset & Dorset throughout	10.9.1863
Clifton Maybank Spur (Yeovil)	13.6.1864
Bristol to Avonmouth Dock	6.3.1865
West Somerset Mineral Railway	4.9.1865
Creech to Chard	11.9.1866
Bristol to Portishead	18.4.1867
Mangotsfield to Bath	4.8.1869
Yatton to Wells	5.4.1870
Norton Fitzwarren to Wiveliscombe	8.6.1871
Bristol Harbour Railway	11.3.1872
Bristol & North Somerset	3.9.1873
Wiveliscombe to Barnstaple	1.11.1873
Watchet to Minehead	16.7.1874
S & D Bath Extension	20.7.1874
Clifton Extension Railway	1.10.1874
Kingswood Junc to Ashley Hill	1.10.1874
Clifton Extension Railway	24.2.1877
Avonmouth Docks	24.2.1877
Hallatrow to Camerton	1.3.1882
Edington to Bridgewater	21.7.1890
Weston, Clevedon & Portishead	1.12.1897
Avonmouth to Pilning Junction	5.2.1900
Wrington Vale Light Railway	4.12.1901
Wootton Bassett to Patchway	1.5.1903
Castle Cary to Langport	2.7.1906
Camerton to Limpley Stoke	9.5.1910

SECTION ONE

Bath to Wellington

THE AREA OF AVON AND SOMERSET has been the subject of numerous boundary revisions over the years, and it is sometimes difficult to describe exactly the allegiance of a particular location at a given point in time. Such is the case with the Georgian city of Bath, a place steeped in history, through which Brunel took his Great Western Railway on its route between London and Bristol.

THE EXTERIOR FAÇADE OF BATH STATION complete with taxis. The photograph was taken in April 1931 and includes a motley selection of early taxis as well as vehicles from the Empire and Christopher Hotels which would meet the trains as required.

AN UNIDENTIFIED 'STAR' CLASS 4–6–0 approaches Bath from the east while a Churchward 'Mogul' waits to depart with a train of LSWR stock. To the right is a short stub siding leading to a wagon turntable, the cramped station site meaning that the station goods yard was a little distance west of the passenger station. (H. Patterson Rutherford)

IT WAS NOT JUST IN THE MAIN STREETS that the city's famed stone-faced buildings might be found. This backwater leading onto the railway is typical of the eastern suburbs. (H. Patterson Rutherford)

WEST OF BATH towards Bristol was Saltford station. This view looks towards the 176 yd Saltford Tunnel and Bristol. The layout here is an indication of the existence of the former broad gauge, witnessed by the space available between the two running lines. (Lens of Sutton)

KEYNSHAM STATION looking west towards Bristol. The ornate design of the footbridge was typical of those found on the lines of the GWR and is complete with decorative scrolls. (Lens of Sutton)

SEEN FROM THE OPPOSITE DIRECTION, again with the wide gap between the running lines. In keeping with a number of other locations, this was later reduced by the simple expedient of widening the passenger platforms (see previous view). There was an extensive goods yard at Keynsham, which was located towards Bath beyond the passenger station. Years later Keynsham would become implanted upon the minds of a generation when a commercial radio station ran a long series of adverts on a certain 'infallible' method of winning the pools. Punters were invited to write to the advertiser at an address described as 'K-E-Y-N, S-H-A-MMMM', Keynshammm, Bristol . . . (Lens of Sutton)

A VENTILATION SHAFT FOR ST ANNE'S TUNNEL which was 1,017 yd long. These were usually surmounted by brick and stone to reduce danger to people on top of the tunnel, while the top was often finished off with castellations in contemporary style.

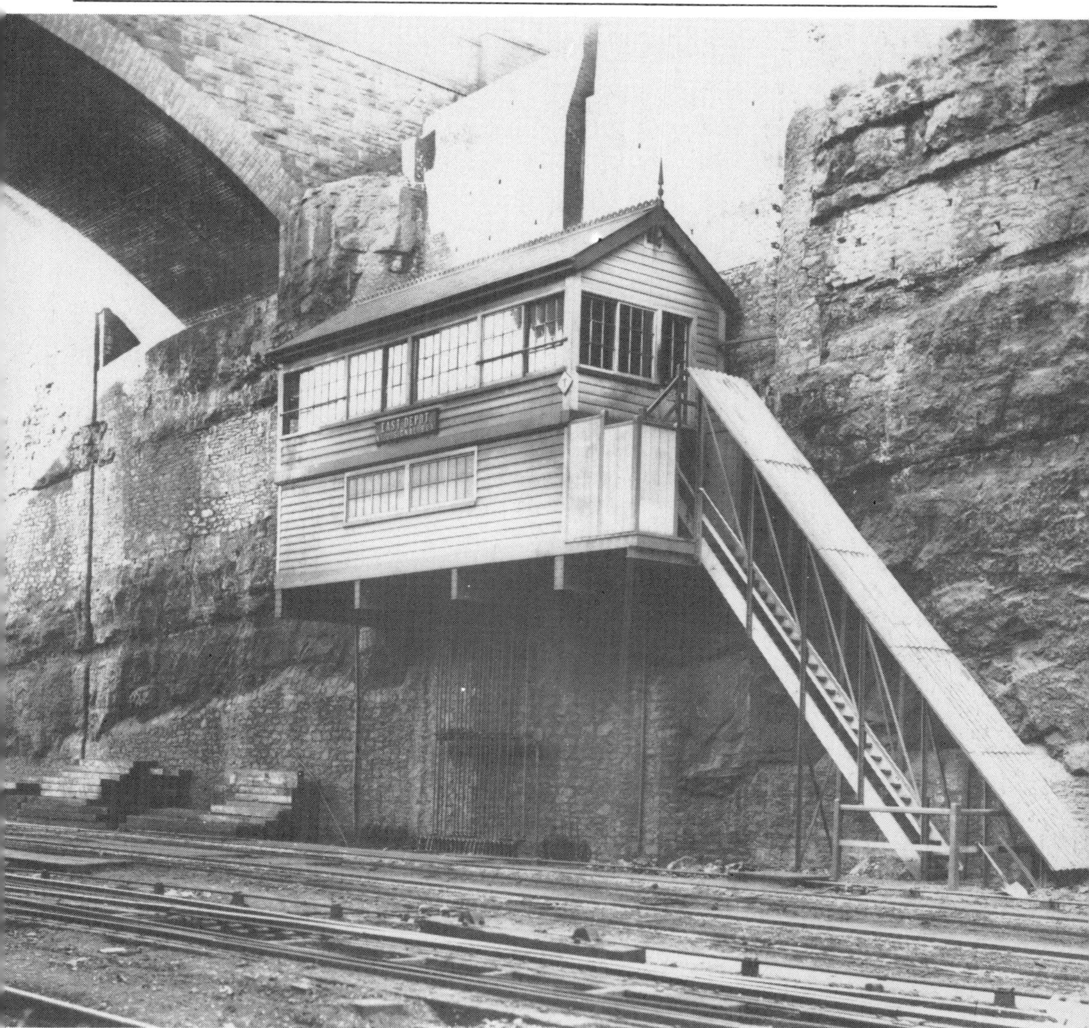

THE RAILWAY'S APPROACH TO BRISTOL from the east was via a deep cutting, which opened out into a fan of sidings on both sides of the main line. Partly controlling the entry and exit from these sidings was 'East Depot No. 2 Signal Box', which because of restricted space had to be located against the rock face of the cutting. Accordingly large girders were positioned in the cutting side. While the box itself is now a memory, the stub ends of the supporting girders remain. (GWR)

THE LONDON END OF BRISTOL TEMPLE MEADS STATION, purportedly taken on 24 August 1924. To the left is the cavernous roof of the main train shed, still in use today, taking the main line south towards Bridgwater and Taunton. Straight ahead is the terminus of the original main line from London, which in recent years has seen a change from railway use, becoming first a car park before restoration work commenced on what is a splendid example of Victorian engineering.

A CLOSE-UP OF THE ENTRANCE TO THE MAIN TRAIN SHED, taken from the east. Bristol was quickly to become the meeting point for two lines, the GWR and Bristol and Exeter routes, the latter soon absorbed by the GWR. The curved station marked a connection between the two concerns. In typical railway fashion it was extended further in an *ad hoc* manner until modernized by the GWR in the 1930s.

SEEN FROM THE WEST END with what was later known as the fish dock area to the left. The sharp curves and covered-in trackwork are obvious, as are the semaphore signals which disappeared from Bristol very early on, being replaced by an early system of power signalling.

'SAINT CLASS 4–6–0, No. 2986 *Robin Hood* outside the huge west signal box at Bristol. (HMRS)

SEEN FROM THE CONNECTING FOOTBRIDGE inside the main station, a number of trains are visible. Also apparent is the nowadays unusual feature of the double-sided platform faces, which were intended to allow pasengers to alight from one side and join from the other, thereby speeding up station work. (Lens of Sutton)

A FINAL VIEW INSIDE THE MAIN STATION, this time with an interloper visible, in the form of a Midland Railway train. Both the platform and track layout were later altered with access between the platforms superseded by a subway, which still survives. (Lens of Sutton)

FOLLOWING THE REMODELLING AND RESIGNALLING of the layout, control at Bristol was exercised from two main power boxes. This view shows the east signal box together with some of its 'searchlight' colour light signals. (GWR)

THE EQUALLY IMPRESSIVE WEST SIGNAL BOX which survived until the area was re-signalled with multiple aspect signalling. To the right is the separate relay room which housed the main electrical work for the power signalling. Both structures have had their lower window openings removed and bricked up, which assists in dating the photograph as post-1945.

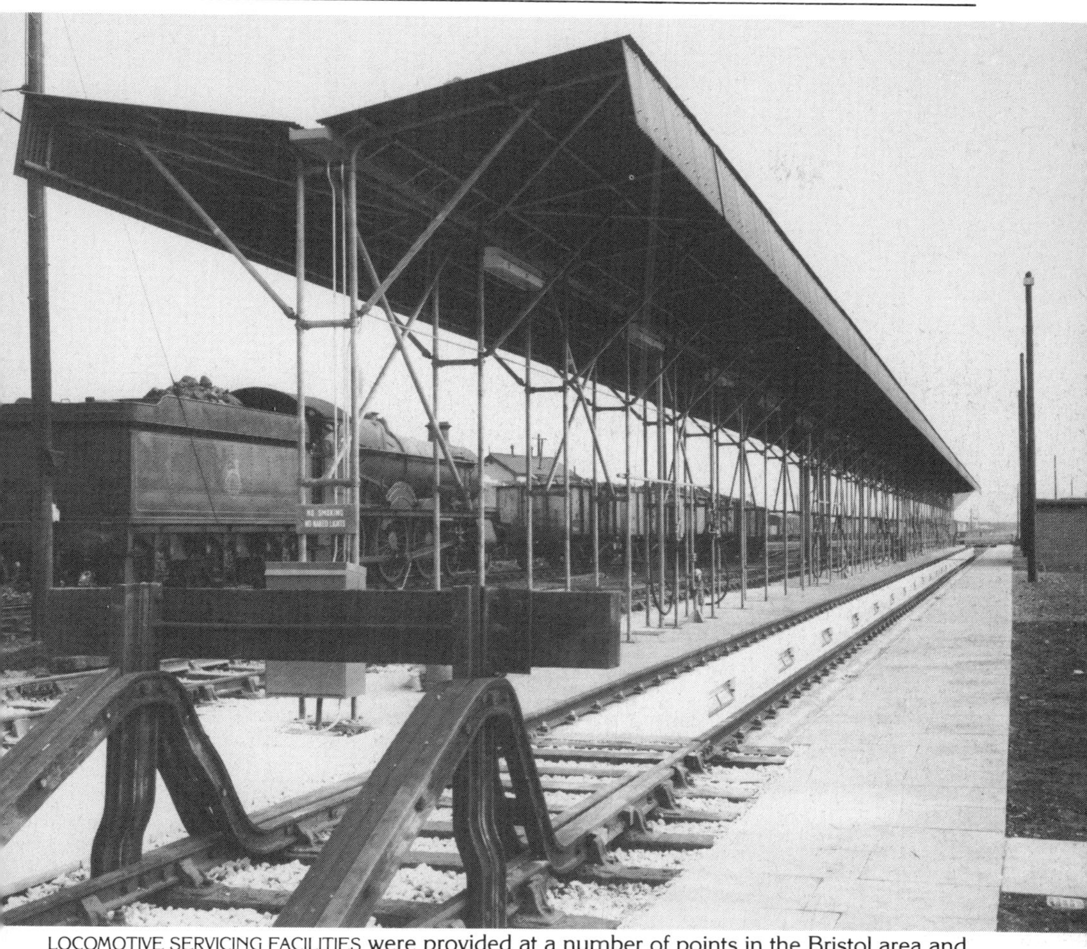

LOCOMOTIVE SERVICING FACILITIES were provided at a number of points in the Bristol area and were later supplemented with facilities for diesel traction. One of the first of these was the re-fuelling point at Marsh Junction which, despite its clean inspection pits, was still exposed to the elements in time-honoured steam fashion. Forming a background to the photograph is No. 4909 *Blakesley Hall*.

THE RURAL RAILWAY. Dean goods No. 2526 near Bristol at the head of a two coach local working.

FLAX BOURTON STATION was south of Bristol towards Taunton, just over 124 miles from Paddington. This was the first station to serve the locality and at the time was known as Bourton. A replacement station was later provided a little further south. Notice the mixed gauge track and complex pointwork which is useful in dating the photograph as pre-1892. (Lens of Sutton)

AS A COMPARISON here is the second station at Flax Bourton with buildings and other structures in typical GWR style. By this time the broad gauge track had been removed. The view looks north towards Bristol. (Lens of Sutton)

AN EXTERIOR VIEW of the junction station at Yatton which was the changing point for passengers destined for Clevedon, the Cheddar Valley and Wrington Vale lines – of which more later. The milk churns are an obvious feature. Many stations originally dealt with this type of traffic, which has now been totally lost to road transport. (Lens of Sutton)

THE WEST END OF YATTON STATION with the Clevedon branch train and junction on the left. On the right it is also just possible to discern a Cheddar Valley service although the engine is obscured by the signal gantry. Notice also the four- and six-wheeled passenger coaches in the yard by the goods shed. (Lens of Sutton)

LOOKING NORTH through the main platforms at Yatton reveals the differing canopy designs. That on the left is a throwback to the days of the original Bristol and Exeter Company, while to the right the eliptical arch is more reminiscent of contemporary London & South Western practice. (Lens of Sutton)

A FINAL VIEW OF THE STATION included to show the diminutive ground frame cabin on the 'Down' platform just beneath the footbridge. This was provided to operate a cross-over at the north end of the station which was otherwise considered too far for control from the main signal box. Such ground frame cabins were once a common feature of GWR practice. (Lens of Sutton)

SEVEN MILES SOUTH OF YATTON was Weston-super-Mare, renowned as 'a seaside watering hole', and originally served by a short branch running at right angles to the main line. This was superseded from 1884 with what became known as the Weston-super-Mare loop which, as the name implies, left the main line at Worle and rejoined it again at Uphill Junction. It survives to this day. As might be expected the station at Weston is built on a curve and is seen to advantage here as one of the magnificent Dean single-wheelers enters the station with a train bound for Bristol.

AS A COMPARISON here is a view of the original terminus at Weston. It can be located by the distant view of the later station on the extreme left. The original site was used almost entirely for goods traffic although it would still see passenger trains in the form of excursion traffic at the height of the summer season. (Lens of Sutton)

THE WESTON LOOP rejoined the main line at Uphill Junction with a signal box provided to control movements at this point. Taken on 6 July 1932, the photograph shows signalman Lance Robshaw on the right.

A VIEW TOWARDS UPHILL JUNCTION showing the two water towers provided for 'Up' and 'Down' lines. The signals referred to the routes to Weston and Bristol. Their equal height implied each route was as important as the other.

A FINAL VIEW OF THE JUNCTION taken from the bridge visible in the previous view. In the foreground is a sleeper-built platelayer's hut complete with the stone grinding wheel used by the men to sharpen their scythes and rip hooks. In the far distance it is just possible to make out another train in the 'Down' siding.

SOUTH OF UPHILL JUNCTION was the station of Bleadon and Uphill, renamed from its previous designation of Uphill. Fortunately the locality was well recorded by contemporary photographers and the first view in this series shows a 'Down' Exeter express passing through the station around the turn of the century, headed by a Dean single. Despite the presence of the train the attention of the staff is directed towards the photographer who has done well to capture the entire scene including the movement of the train. (Lens of Sutton)

THE STATION BUILDINGS at Bleadon and Uphill with what may well be the station master's house behind. The photograph shows the various structures to have been provided on an add-on basis, with only one, on the extreme left, representing true GWR design. (Lens of Sutton)

A BUSY TIME AT THE STATION with a double-headed Exeter express passing a northbound goods. The signals at the end of the platform control the main line to Uphill Junction, with the distant signal on the left allowing free passage to Weston when in the 'off' position. All the signal arms are painted red – yellow was not used until after 1927. The narrow platform is again obvious. (Lens of Sutton)

PRESUMABLY TAKEN AT THE SAME TIME as the previous view – from the location of the toy animal on the platform – this time the engine is a Dean 4–4–0 and resplendant in spotless livery. If only we had had the benefit of colour photography ninety years ago. (Lens of Sutton)

CONCLUDING THIS SEQUENCE on the station is a view looking south and an interesting collection of vehicles making up the 'Down' train. Those identifiable include a horse box, a syphon van (used for milk), a 40 ft passenger brake van and clerestory coaches. The high-roofed vehicle next to the engine, however, is a mystery. (Lens of Sutton)

RUNNING ALMOST DUE SOUTH the main Bristol and Exeter route reached Highbridge, where the rival Somerset and Dorset Railway also had a station. Photos of the S & D in this area will be found in the final section of the book. This heavily retouched view looks north and makes for an interesting comparison with the later BR view of the station. (Lens of Sutton)

AS MENTIONED IN THE SECTION ON YATTON, the railways were for many years the principal carrier of milk to the London creameries, with churns gathered from a wide area. One of the stations involved with this traffic was Highbridge where, in 1928, the photographer has captured a horse-dray, belonging to the Highbridge Bacon Company, loading churns into a syphon. The slatted sides of the syphon van were designed to allow the flow of cool air while the train was running.

A COMPARISON CAN BE MADE between the earlier view of the station (opposite) and this photograph of BR days. On this occasion it is a 'Hall' class locomotive passing through. Another obvious difference is that the platform has now been rendered and paving stones added. The view was one of a series made in 1958 when Highbridge featured in the Western Region magazine under the heading, 'Spotlight on Highbridge'.

SOUTH OF HIGHBRIDGE, the main line passes through Durston. Here 57xx pannier tank No. 5771 is caught in the act of shunting wagons in the 'Down' sidings. As well as the steam engine, the shunter with his long pole and the telegraph poles are features now rarely seen, and yet the photograph was taken in the comparatively recent 1950s. Beyond Durston the 'Up' and 'Down' lines parted company briefly, as can be seen through the overbridge. This was to allow the down line to climb the flyover taking the Bristol and Exeter across the top of the Somerton cut-off at Cogload Junction. North of Durston a single line loop ran east towards Athelney.

THE PRINCIPAL STATION between Bristol and Exeter was Taunton, which can hardly have justice done to it in the space of a few photographs. The reader is referred to the accompanying book in this series dealing with the town itself. As far as the railway was concerned there were four tracks through the station as well as a west loop used by freight traffic and, of course, yards and locomotive facilities. To match the importance of the station an imposing main building was provided and is seen here from the approach with a motley collection of 1950s road vehicles. (Lens of Sutton)

I COULD NOT RESIST THE INCLUSION OF THIS VIEW OF THE STATION INTERIOR, complete with express service, in spite of slightly sub-standard quality. The silhouettes of the two men on the platform provide an interesting balance to the photograph. (Lens of Sutton)

LIKE BRISTOL, Taunton was one of the sites greatly extended by the GWR in later years to remove what was a traffic bottleneck. The overall roof was replaced by canopies and four through platform faces were also provided. All survive today although only two are in regular use. Taunton was also the terminus for trains on both the Minehead and Barnstaple branches even though the junctions for both of these were some few miles further west. (Lens of Sutton)

THE EFFECT OF ADVERSE WEATHER CONDITIONS at Creech St Michael, near Taunton. Regretfully the date is not reported. Water can be seen swirling up almost to the level of the carriage footboards and it is a wonder the engine fire was not also affected. (Collection R.S. Carpenter)

THE ORIGINAL STATION AT WELLINGTON, showing the staff paused from their duties for the benefit of the photographer. Westbound trains would be faced with a stiff climb from the station for some distance until reaching White Ball tunnel, which marked the division between Somerset and Devon. (Lens of Sutton)

IN LATER YEARS Wellington station was rebuilt with passing loops either side of the 'Up' and 'Down' platforms although the view here is prior to the rebuilding. Again the Bristol and Exeter railway architecture is apparent with its all-round canopy in the distinct Brunel style. (Lens of Sutton)

A FINAL VIEW OF THE STATION from the vantage point of the overbridge. Notice the staggered platforms and also the tall home signal – the latter's height was dictated by the need to be visible to trains from the approach side of the overbridge. (Lens of Sutton)

SECTION TWO

Bristol to Winterbourne

THE STATION AT LAWRENCE HILL in the Bristol suburbs on the line north from Dr Day's Bridge junction. This was originally part of the Bristol and South Wales Union line towards the pier at New Passage, although it was not until takeover by the GWR and subsequent expansion that four platforms were provided. (Lens of Sutton)

WITH THE STATION DEVOID OF TRAINS it is possible to glimpse the impressive facilities provided. Notice the plethora of advertisements typical of the period, as well as the items of contemporary station furniture. The line here was on a steep gradient north towards Filton, which called for care in the working of trains over the route. (Lens of Sutton)

STAPLETON ROAD JUNCTION was also on the line towards Filton and, as the name implies, was the junction for Clifton and Avonmouth. Again, the advertisements are worthy of a second glance as are the two porters intent on the inspection of the luggage mounted on the barrow. (Lens of Sutton)

A BUSY SCENE AT STAPLETON ROAD, with milk churns on the platform, unusual perhaps for an urban station. This was one of the commuter stations in the Bristol area, with two of the platforms reserved for local and branch line services. (Lens of Sutton)

LOOKING SOUTH through the station at Stapleton Road, with the tail end of a main line service disappearing from view. Already in this Edwardian scene urban development has encroached almost to the boundary fence. Today the station has long since ceased to exist in the form depicted here. (Lens of Sutton)

A STEAM RAILMOTOR entering the platform at Ashley Hill station near Bristol, complete with a trailing carriage in tow. Notice the open top station footbridge which was an unusual feature on a Great Western line. (Lens of Sutton)

A DELIGHTFUL STUDY OF A GIRLS' OUTING at Ashley Hill, posed for the camera. How long such dresses would remain clean on the footbridge is uncertain! In the left background it is just possible to discern the station signal box, while the hanging board under the footbridge proclaims, 'Passengers are requested TO CROSS the line by the BRIDGE'. (Lens of Sutton)

PART OF THE COMPLEX LAYOUT AT FILTON JUNCTION which was basically a diamond shape with additional lines crossing the middle. In the distance is one of the signal boxes used to control the junction, while near at hand is a superb example of an early GWR wooden bracket signal. (Mowat Collection)

NORTH-WEST FROM FILTON was the station at Patchway which was on the line leading towards the Severn Tunnel. The station shown here dated from the opening of the direct line through Badminton in 1903, and was built by the same contractor, Messrs Pearsons. (Lens of Sutton)

THE ORIGINAL LINE NORTH FROM BRISTOL was built by the Bristol and South Wales Union Company and was originally a single line of rails. This was later taken over by the GWR and doubled to form part of the direct approach to the Severn Tunnel. This doubling included the section at Patchway where there was a single bore tunnel which for various reasons was not opened out. Instead a separate line was built on a slightly different level nearby. The photograph illustrates the difference in levels well, and shows No. 7021 *Haverfordwest Castle* near Patchway Tunnel signal box in August 1950 with a South Wales to Paddington express. (Collection R.S. Carpenter)

TO CATER FOR GOODS TRAFFIC to and from South Wales an expansive goods yard was laid out on land at Stoke Gifford consequent upon the opening of the direct line through Badminton. This view is from the east end and shows some of the sidings as well as, in the distance, the platforms of the new Bristol Parkway station added by BR many years later. (C.G. Maggs)

A COMMON FEATURE OF THE GWR was to brand vehicles to a particular depot. This 'toad' – the telegraphic code name for a goods brake van – has been allocated to Stoke Gifford although the picture was clearly not taken at that location.

AN UNIDENTIFIED 'SAINT' CLASS 4–6–0 on a stopping service near Stoke Gifford. The motley collection of stock was typical of many GWR trains and indeed the uniform four coach rake at the start could be said to be unusual.

NEAR STOKE GIFFORD is No. 4924 *Eydon Hall* with a running in turn. The vehicles would appear to be a 'B' set, which were in regular use on local services throughout the system.

THE TYPICAL, ALTHOUGH OFTEN UNPHOTOGRAPHED SIDE OF RAILWAY WORKING, a local goods service in charge of Dean goods 0–6–0 No. 2567 between Winterbourne and Stoke Gifford.

EAST FROM STOKE GIFFORD towards Chipping Sodbury, Badminton and eventually Paddington, was Winterbourne station. Nowadays the line is still open at this point although the station has long ceased to exist even though there is now considerable residential development in the area. Notice the change from masonry to timber for the platforms, which provided for cheapness in construction. (Mowat Collection)

CHURCHWARD 'STAR' CLASS 4–6–0, No. 4041 *Prince of Wales* at the head of a London-bound express near Winterbourne in the 1930s. The engine is attached to a large 4,000 gallon tender although still retaining its small Churchward cab.

TAKEN FROM THE SAME VANTAGE POINT although this time with No. 4099 *Kilgerran Castle* at the head of the train. This particular engine was built in 1926 and withdrawn in 1962 having covered over 1.8 million miles. A full history of the route through Badminton and Winterbourne is available in my book *GWR: The Badminton Line*.

SECTION THREE

Frome to Athelney

MOVING SOUTH, we join the route of the former Wilts., Somerset and Weymouth Railway at Frome. Once typical of many GWR stations, the wooden overall roof gradually fell out of favour and most were removed. Frome, however, has managed to retain this feature although regretfully the track layout is much simplified and pannier tanks no longer call at the station.

THE ORIGINAL COURSE of the Wilts., Somerset and Weymouth Railway took in Frome, although an avoiding line was built in the 1930s leaving the original station situated on what was now a loop. (Lens of Sutton)

A VIEW FROM THE EAST END OF THE STATION with the main road passing underneath the railway via the girder bridge. Frome was once the junction for the North Somerset line towards Radstock and Bristol although nowadays this only extends as far as a mineral quarry. (Lens of Sutton)

A ROYAL VISITOR TO FROME in 1966; HRH The Duke of Edinburgh being greeted at the station on the occasion of his visit to Somerset. The dark interior of the station, due to the overall roof, is apparent and was one of the reasons for the unpopularity and removal of this feature at other stations.

WEST OF FROME was the station at Bruton which still survives today although minus its station buildings. Close examination of the view reveals several milk churns and a passenger apparently engaged in re-tying his boot lace. (Lens of Sutton)

FROM THE STATION FOOTBRIDGE, the photograph looks east towards the small yard, just visible under the overbridge. Again, the gap between the tracks is a throwback to broad gauge days. It is possible to see the neat and tidy platform gardens, once a common feature of so many country stations.

DESPITE BEING BOMBED at a number of locations in the 1940s, the GWR were fortunate in losing just two engines as a direct result of enemy action, one of these, No. 1729, at Castle Cary in September 1942. Quite why the Somerset town should have received the attention of the enemy in favour of more attractive targets is uncertain although it was very unfortunate for the station as besides the damaged engine the signal box was also destroyed and there were a number of casualties.

HAPPIER TIMES AT CASTLE CARY with No. 5074 *Hampden* passing through with the 'Down' 'Torbay Express'. Castle Cary was also the junction for the original line to Weymouth via Yeovil which diverged from the Taunton route behind the photographer.

THE LINE FROM CASTLE CARY TO LANGPORT was built as one of the cut-off routes intended to shorten the distance to the west and was not opened until 1906. Several new stations appeared on the line including that at Keinton Mandeville seen here. Although still open as part of the main line to the west, this country station has long since ceased to exist.

A DELIGHTFUL VIEW of the signal box at Keinton Mandeville with two members of staff posed by the steps. The humble mechanical signal box is a fast-disappearing species and this example is now consigned to the history books. The signal man would often make his own box very much a home-from-home, with plants inside. The large windows made for ideal greenhouse conditions. Despite these advantages signal boxes could also be draughty locations and here an attempt has been made to reduce the chill with an amount of timber at the exit of the rodding and wire runs. (Lens of Sutton)

BEING A RELATIVELY RECENT LINE – it was opened in 1906 – photographs have survived showing the construction of the route through Somerton towards Langport. This view, taken shortly before the work was completed, shows the station buildings in the final stages of construction while a works train waits in the platform. (Lens of Sutton)

SEVERE FLOODING AT LANGPORT STATION in 1887 with the tracks under almost 3 ft of water. Under these circumstances it is unlikely much traffic would be moving, although a group of staff and passengers are waiting expectantly on the platform.

SEEN FROM THE OPPOSITE DIRECTION the extent of the floods are apparent. Besides this obvious feature there are a number of other items worthy of study in this early view, including the marooned wagons in the yard, slotted post signal and station furniture. The water crane would seem to a be a superfluous addition to the scene.

LIKE THE OTHER STOPPING PLACES ON THE ROUTE from Castle Cary to Taunton, that at Athelney is now but a memory, although this signal box did survive until comparatively recent times. Again the railwaymen are posed for the camera, and a glance through the open window of the signal box reveals the top half of a Webb & Thompson staff instrument used for controlling movement on the single line spur to Durston. (Lens of Sutton)

I COULD NOT RESIST THE INCLUSION OF THESE TWO DELIGHTFUL VIEWS of the rural scene near Athelney in August 1920, recorded by the GWR official photographer. Taken with a plate frame camera the detail shows up well, including the motorcyclist, pedal cyclists and dog, as well as the villagers themselves. (GWR)

SECTION FOUR

Yatton and Yeovil

MOVING AWAY FROM THE MAIN ROUTES to the branch lines and Yatton, where a GWR design diesel railcar swings away from the Bristol and Exeter route bound for Clevedon. Diesel railcars were in use on the GWR from the early 1930s and were the forerunners of today's multiple unit trains. (Lens of Sutton)

THE OTHER BRANCH FROM YATTON was that south-east towards Cheddar and eventually Witham with the first station on the line at Congresbury. This was also the junction for another branch to Blagdon which diverged at the far end of the station. (Lens of Sutton)

BUSY TIMES AT CONGRESBURY with what appears to be the Yatton train and a goods train occupying the platforms. The line here was double through the station and single for the rest of its route, the goods having been shunted to allow the passenger to pass. (Lens of Sutton)

A LITTLE OVER FOUR MILES FROM CONGRESBURY towards Blagdon was the station at Langford seen here from across some rather well cultivated allotments. Besides the main buildings there is an ornate cast-iron toilet on the platform. A similar structure is preserved and still in use at Bewdley on the Severn Valley Railway. (Lens of Sutton)

THE STATION AT LANGFORD is well covered photographically considering the obscurity of the railway, and here it is seen from the opposite end. The light trackwork of the line is apparent as is the 'spear' fencing which was a common feature throughout the GWR system. (Lens of Sutton)

IN THIS, THE FINAL VIEW OF THE LOCATION, the station maintains its tidy appearance. Two members of staff are visible together with a lady and child. Notice the neat station gardens, which would have been cultivated by the staff as part of their daily duties. (Lens of Sutton)

THE TERMINUS OF THE LINE AT BLAGDON, six and a half miles from Congresbury. The station was situated in a cutting some little way from the village of the same name. Notice the single carriage in the small yard, of the type used for camping at a variety of locations. (Lens of Sutton)

THE LAYOUT AT BLAGDON STATION was basic yet functional, consisting of a passing loop and small goods yard, all of which were laid with light flat bottom rail as seen here. Again the station has a cast-iron privy on the platform while behind this is a grounded coach body used as additional storage accommodation. (Lens of Sutton)

BLAGDO

SEEN FROM THE END OF THE RUN ROUND LOOP the similarity in design to the building at Langford is obvious as is the number of staff for this little railway. In the background an engine is in the process of shunting a number of six-wheeled coaches in the yard which may indicate that the photograph was taken at the start or end of the day's service. (Lens of Sutton)

Previous page:
TAKEN AROUND THE TIME THE LINE WAS OPENED in 1901 this stunning view gives a panorama of the terminus. Notice the siding full of private owner wagons belonging to John Wainwright & Company, Moons Hill Quarry, Cranmore, as well as the contractor's vehicles behind. The line was built by contractor Herbert Weldon from Birmingham. His wagons are in the siding behind waiting to be cleared following completion of the work.

RETURNING NOW TO THE CHEDDAR VALLEY BRANCH and south from Congresbury to Axbridge. Here the station was slightly above the level of the town as the line climbed towards Congresbury. (Lens of Sutton)

THE NARROWING OF THE GAUGE has resulted in a wide gap between the two running lines. Axbridge was a station with all the charm of the rural railway, its milk churns marked with the location name, just one example of how the railways were once the prime carrier of traffic throughout the land. (Lens of Sutton)

ONE OF THE PRINCIPAL PRODUCTS FOR TRANSPORT from the station was rabbit; another was soft fruit during what was a short season. Accordingly the transit of this produce was a priority to the railway. A train load of ventilated syphon vans is drawn up at the platform and ready to be loaded. (Lens of Sutton)

A FINAL VIEW OF AXBRIDGE STATION, looking south-east towards Cheddar. The main buildings are constructed in a chalet style and mirror those seen on another West Country branch line running through the Exe Valley. Trains no longer run between the platforms; instead it is a main road, bypassing the village that uses the formation. The buildings and goods shed still remain. I wonder how many road users are aware of what existed there some years before. (Lens of Sutton)

CHEDDAR was another of the stations to possess an overall roof and is seen here in broad gauge days purportedly with its first train arriving. If this is the case then the view is quite remarkable. It does show the extreme width of the broad gauge to advantage as well as some of the contemporary fashions of the period.

A LATER VIEW OF THE STATION still with its overall roof. The group of men would appear to be engaged in replacing sleepers – a hard and thankless task, essential to the safe running of the railway. The dingy interior of the train shed is apparent as is the 'uniform' of the permanent way gang, each with waistcoat and watch chain.

THE BRANCH TRAIN AT CHEDDAR. Although depicted in BR days this scene changed little over the years. No. 4595 is in pristine external condition and the station too looks smart in rough stone with ornate barge boards. (Lens of Sutton)

ALTHOUGH ONLY BUILT FOR A SINGLE LINE OF RAILS, the earthworks on the Cheddar Valley line were generally of sufficient width to take a second line had this ever been required, with the same specification applied to a number of the bridges. This feature shows up well here at Wookey station where the overbridge covers not only the single line but the platform as well. (Lens of Sutton)

FROM ONCE BEING ABLE TO BOAST TWO RAILWAY STATIONS on separate routes, Shepton Mallet is now devoid of rail communication, both the Cheddar Valley and Somerset & Dorset routes but a memory. To distinguish between the two stations BR designated the former GWR station 'High Street', which addition can be seen on the station name board. Notice also the staggered platforms which were necessary due to the proximity of the goods shed and yard to the station. (Lens of Sutton)

FROM THE OPPOSITE END OF THE STATION the two tracks can be seen converging into one beneath the overbridge which again has provision for a second line of rails. Apart from the boy under the canopy the station is particularly devoid of patronage which would later result in the closure of the line to all traffic. (Lens of Sutton)

DAMAGE TO AN UNDERBRIDGE AT SHEPTON MALLET in October 1941, presumably as a result of enemy action. The exposure of the crown of the arch reveals the method of construction: an outer skin of bricks supporting stone blocks. The railway was later repaired and restored to normal use.

NOW THE HEADQUARTERS OF THE EAST SOMERSET RAILWAY, Cranmore station was located near several stone quarries, a feature of this part of Somerset. Since 1970 the firm of Foster Yeoman has operated a large stone quarry nearby, which means rail access has survived between the East Somerset route and BR at what was formerly the junction station at Witham on the main line. (Lens of Sutton)

AT YEOVIL the GWR and LSWR systems met and evolved into a complexity of lines and junctions many of which survived until rationalized by BR. As far as the GWR was concerned Yeovil was on the direct route from Castle Cary to Weymouth, and here a 'Down' Weymouth express is passing Clifton Maybank Junction behind a 'Bulldog' class 4–4–0 in 1908. (Collection R.S. Carpenter)

A SUPERB VIEW INSIDE THE TRAIN SHED at the GWR station of Yeovil Pen Mill, where passengers were invited to change for the line to Durston and Taunton. The two-sided platform still survives as does the footbridge, although the overall roof is now long gone. (Lens of Sutton)

BESIDES THEIR OWN INDIVIDUAL STATIONS AT YEOVIL, the GWR and SR shared the use of the town station at the end of which the routes forked, the left continuing towards Pen Mill, that to the right leading towards Yeovil Junction. (Lens of Sutton)

RETAINING ITS SINGLE PLATFORM FACES, Yeovil Pen Mill changed little over the years as this scene from the 1950s shows. The pannier tank is probably on a local train to Taunton. The nameboard invites passengers to change for Exeter even if this will involve a further change at Taunton and a journey of over one and a half hours. For those in the know there was a direct link to Exeter from the SR station at Yeovil Junction, which took half the time! (Lens of Sutton)

A PANORAMIC VIEW of the locomotive facilities and yard at Yeovil Town, with an amount of LSWR stock visible. The photograph was taken from a footpath and shows what used to be the turntable road nearest the camera as well as a neat coal stack laid down in case of fuel shortage. (Lens of Sutton)

YEOVIL PEN MILL in Great Western days with a 'Bulldog' class engine on what is probably a stopping service to Weymouth. (Lens of Sutton)

FORMER LSWR L11 CLASS 4–4–0, NO. 407 between duties at Yeovil Town shed in Southern days. The design of the shed here was unusual, being in brick throughout rather than just the sides. Notice the large smoke ducts running the length of the roof as well as the ventilators in the ends. (Lens of Sutton)

A DELIGHTFUL RURAL SCENE. Dean goods No. 2543 near Yeovil in August 1928. The unspoilt countryside at this point belies the complexity of the railway layout at the Somerset town. (Lens of Sutton)

ANOTHER STOP ON THE ROYAL VISIT of 1957 was Yeovil. The Duke of Edinburgh is seen alighting at Yeovil Pen Mill to be greeted by various dignitaries including the mayor of the town.

A FINAL VIEW OF YEOVIL, this time back to the Town station which has now lost its overall roof. Following a change in boundaries, Yeovil Town came under full control of the SR which resulted in a hotchpotch of features including a number of upper quadrant signals, one of these seen immediately to the left of the engine. Following closure the site was used as a stopping point for long distance coaches and has now been completely redeveloped. (Lens of Sutton)

SITUATED ON THE SINGLE BRANCH LINE from Yeovil Town towards Langport, Montacute station was one of four stopping places. There was no passing place at the station although, as can be seen, a signal box and signals were provided. (Lens of Sutton)

SECTION FIVE

West of Taunton

WEST OF TAUNTON the lines to Barnstaple and Minehead diverged at Norton Fitzwarren station, with Wiveliscombe on the former route. This was a single line branch with passing loops at the stations. Local stone was used for much of the construction at Wiveliscombe and the architecture of the main buildings is unique to this particular railway.

WEST OF WIVELISCOMBE the Barnstaple branch traverses part of north Devon before a re-arrangement of boundaries takes it once more into Somerset just prior to Dulverton station. This was nominally just a passing place on the single line branch, although Dulverton also served as the junction station for trains on the Exe Valley branch which diverged east of the station at Morebath Junction. Consequently the layout of the facilities was extensive and viewed from the hill they give the impression of a busy railway location. (Lens of Sutton)

AN ALMOST EMPTY VIEW OF THE STATION which shows to advantage the layout and number of sidings available. The photograph makes for an interesting comparison with the next view, especially with regard to the changes to the canopy and buildings. (Lens of Sutton)

FROM THE SAME LOCATION, yet some years earlier, this view of Dulverton shows the station as it appeared around the turn of the century. Despite the existence of the footbridge a number of passengers seem intent on using the board crossing, including a man with several hoops on his shoulder. To the right in the far distance an engine is busy in a yard filled with vehicles, including several private owner wagons. (Lens of Sutton)

TIMBER STACKED IN THE YARD AT DULVERTON in 1923, the railway having provided two fixed yard cranes. Such equipment has almost vanished from the railway scene today. (Lens of Sutton)

MOVING NOW from Norton Fitzwarren to the Minehead branch which, although closed by BR, has been resurrected as the privately operated West Somerset Railway. The view is of Bishops Lydeard station with a Taunton-bound train in, taken from the conveniently placed road overbridge. The station is almost unaltered today and marks the southernmost point of regular operation from Minehead. (Lens of Sutton)

NORTH TOWARDS MINEHEAD and a very early view of Watchet station dating from the time when the railway terminated at this point. The broad gauge trackwork is evident, as is the early disc and cross bar signal and original engine shed. Notice also the multitude of rolling stock in the distance.

SIMILAR TO THE PREVIOUS VIEW but, because of its clarity and very early date, well worthy of inclusion. In comparison with the other photograph, the engine shed doors are closed while on the right a number of quarry wagons, no doubt from the West Somerset mineral railway, can be seen.

THE DELIGHTFULLY NAMED BLUE ANCHOR STATION on the Minehead line hard by the north Somerset coastline. For many years this was a popular destination for holiday traffic and, despite the station now being in private hands, the scene is little altered today, right down to the level crossing at the Minehead end of the platform which is operated by a wheel from the signal box. (Lens of Sutton)

SECTION SIX

Branch and Cross-Country Routes

BETWEEN THE PLATFORMS at the GWR Radstock station. The use of local stone in the station buildings is apparent. Besides stone the other mineral extracted in the area was coal. The signal box at the far end of the platform was the second box on the site (see p. 102). Following closure it was rescued for preservation by the Great Western Society at Didcot where it has been restored to its former glory. (Lens of Sutton)

66534. RADSTOCK VA

THIS PHOTOGRAPH SHOWS THE ORIGINAL TALL WOODEN SIGNAL BOX which probably dated from around the time the line opened. Entering the platform is what appears to be an 0–4–2T on a local service with the first vehicles, a syphon van and passenger brake. Notice the neat and tidy appearance of the station gardens and the ladies' fashion of the period. (Lens of Sutton)

Previous page:
A SUPERB STUDY OF RADSTOCK STATION on the GWR North Somerset line from Frome to Bristol. Radstock once boasted two stations, one on the GWR route and the other on the erstwhile Somerset and Dorset system between Bath and Bournemouth. Both, alas, are now gone and with them the monumental chaos caused by the road level crossings in the area.

A FINAL VIEW OF RADSTOCK STATION with another long lost feature, namely the wooden walkway between the tracks. This was often provided to aid staff whose duties required them to walk between trains, and would also act as a cover to point rodding. (Lens of Sutton)

ONE OF THE NOTORIOUS LEVEL CROSSINGS AT RADSTOCK which were dispensed with following closure of the railway. The lack of vehicular traffic makes it hard to appreciate the difficulties caused to road vehicles. (Lens of Sutton)

NORTH OF RADSTOCK the railway reaches Hallatrow station, for some years a simple station with one platform. Following the opening of the Camerton branch the station was rebuilt and enlarged as can be seen in the next view. (Lens of Sutton)

ALTHOUGH IT IS SUFFERING FROM DETERIORATION I could not resist the inclusion of this view showing the station at Hallatrow immediately after rebuilding. Note the two platforms and junction signals visible at the far end of the station, which allowed trains to continue north to Bristol or east towards Camerton and eventually Limpley Stoke. (Lens of Sutton)

THIS VIEW OF HALLATROW STATION, taken a little later, also looks towards Bristol and shows the water tower provided at the south end of the platforms. A footbridge, however, has yet to be built. (Lens of Sutton)

A FINAL VIEW OF HALLATROW, at the extent of its development, complete with footbridge. An obvious disadvantage of this feature from an operating point of view is that the junction signals are now obscured. From the number of persons on the platform it would appear the arrival of a train is imminent. (Lens of Sutton)

NORTH OF HALLATROW at Clutton station, two lines led off to the delightfully named Fry's Bottom and Greyfield collieries. This explains the number of open wagons visible in the distance. Besides coal, milk was another commodity handled from the area, and three of the old style churns are standing on the platform. (Lens of Sutton)

PRIOR TO JOINING THE MAIN LINE at Marsh Junction South, the branch passed through Brislington station which consisted of a single platform fronted by several sidings. Posed for the camera is the station master and his staff. The little girl may well be the daughter of one of the workers. (Lens of Sutton)

ANOTHER LINE RUNNING TOWARDS BATH AND BRISTOL FROM THE SOUTH was that from Trowbridge, the station at Freshford originally the first within the county of Somerset. The photograph was taken near the adjacent stopping place at Limpley Stoke and probably around the mid-1930s as it shows an almost brand new streamlined GWR railcar, No. 1, on a Weymouth to Bristol service.

A GROUP OF PERMANENT WAY WORKERS AND PAINTERS posed for the camera on Freshford station. Each division maintained its own painters gang who were responsible for the upkeep of the various structures within the area, Freshford coming within the Bristol division. (Lens of Sutton)

LIMPLEY STOKE STATION looking south towards Freshford in the early years of the century. Notice the opening in the platform immediately beneath the signal box which served as an exit for the signal wires and point rodding. The yard would appear to be well occupied with what may well be stone blocks piled on the right-hand side. (Lens of Sutton)

THE JOINT RAILWAY STATION AT AVONMOUTH which was served by a shuttle service from Bristol. Nearby a number of sidings fanned out to serve the various docks, while there were also factories in the vicinity, including an ammonia plant. (Lens of Sutton)

AN EXTERIOR VIEW OF PORTISHEAD STATION which belies its appearance as a busy branch line terminus. Portishead was on the opposite side of the water to Avonmouth. While the distance as the crow flies was little more than two miles, by rail a journey of over fifteen miles was involved. The station was also the terminal of the independent Weston, Clevedon and Portishead line which closed completely in 1940.

A BUSY SCENE AT PORTISHEAD STATION viewed from the end of the line. To the left part of the docks can be seen while the WC & P route referred to above diverged to the right beyond the overbridge. Notice the small goods shed singularly devoid of traffic although wagons abound elsewhere.

PORTISHEAD FROM THE OPPOSITE DIRECTION and still with no vehicles occupying the goods shed. The open ground opposite the station is surprising and may well have been provided for possible expansion. (Lens of Sutton)

ANOTHER GREAT WESTERN BRANCH LINE within Somerset was that from east of Taunton running south towards Chard where the LSWR also had a station. This was a single track route although at Hatch station a loop was provided, surprisingly devoid of a platform. The photograph looks south towards Ilminster and Chard and shows clearly the Brunel style of station building with its all-round canopy. Nearer the camera is the station master and his dog. (Lens of Sutton)

AWAY NOW FROM THE GWR to the former LSWR main line through Somerset on its way from Salisbury to Exeter. Of all the stopping places between the two named locations, the most renowned must surely be that at Templecombe where the Southern route came into contact with the Somerset and Dorset system. There was a considerable interchange of traffic between the two systems and this shows up well here, with a number of passengers awaiting the arrival of the train. (Lens of Sutton)

SOMERSET AND DORSET LINE SERVICES would sometimes run direct to the LSWR station. This Midland Railway 0–6–0 has arrived with a train from the direction of Bath. (Lens of Sutton)

ANOTHER S & D ARRIVAL at the same platform. Notice the milk churns on the platform – milk was a valued traffic in the area – and the 3-link rather than screw coupling to the front of the engine. (Lens of Sutton)

LOOKING THROUGH the LSWR main line station towards London. Visit the scene today and you will find that what was once a thriving railway community has all but vanished, the station a shadow of its former self and only recently re-opened following several years of complete closure. (Lens of Sutton)

THE SAME SCENE some years earlier with the importance of the station reflected in the number of staff visible. (Lens of Sutton)

A DRUMMOND DESIGN 4–4–0 at the west end of Templecombe station in Southern days. The headcode, one disc centrally mounted on the buffer beam and another above the smokebox, applied to west of England trains on the LSWR main line. (Lens of Sutton)

AN EASTBOUND MAIN LINE SERVICE paused at the station in charge of Drummond 'K10' 4–4–0 No. 394. The locomotive retains its firebox cross tubes and smokebox wing plates. Notice the admiring glance from the passenger on the platform. (Lens of Sutton)

A FINAL VIEW OF THE STATION this time looking west towards Exeter. Beyond the platforms was an extensive marshalling and storage yard, while at the far end of the site was a single road engine shed under the administrative control of Yeovil. (Lens of Sutton)

THE STATION OF MILBORNE PORT, west from Templecombe, was typical of the design of the minor stopping places on the route from Salisbury to Exeter. The route between the two points was double throughout and each station boasted its own goods yard, the size of which depended on local need. In recent times the line has been singled, although it now enjoys a considerable amount of traffic and as a result its future appears secure. (Lens of Sutton)

GEOGRAPHICALLY WE HAVE MISSED the stopping place at Sherborne although the excuse for this is that it falls within Dorset. Therefore the next stop on the main line is at Yeovil Junction, the junction designation given to distinguish it from the other stations in the town. The photograph looks east towards Templecombe, the gantry of signals protecting the main line and passenger loop as well as the connection towards stations at Town and Pen Mill which leads off to the left. (Lens of Sutton)

BESIDES THE TWO PLATFORM FACES for main line trains, Yeovil Junction also boasted loop platforms as well as through lines for 'Up' and 'Down' passing traffic. These are seen to the right. The signal box in the distance marks the point of divergence for the Salisbury and Town and Pen Mill routes. (Lens of Sutton)

PART OF THE GOODS YARD at the east end of Yeovil Junction with a variety of wagons visible. In the days when the railway dealt with 'smalls' traffic, there was an amount of shunting carried out at each station. At Yeovil in particular there would be 'trip' working between the three stations. (Lens of Sutton).

LOOKING WEST TOWARDS EXETER with what is probably a local service standing on the far left. Despite the curvature, main line services would be steaming hard at this point as there were a number of fast non-stop trains between Salisbury and Exeter. (Lens of Sutton)

PRIVATE OWNER WAGON from Yeovil gas works.

SUTTON BINGHAM beyond Yeovil, like Milborne Port was a wayside station on a main line. Evidence of milk traffic is apparent as is the care lavished by the station staff on the gardens and flower borders. (Lens of Sutton)

CHARD WAS SERVED BY TWO LINES, the LSWR route from the south coming from Chard junction on the main Exeter line, and the GWR route from near Taunton from the north. Originally each company maintained its own station in close proximity to the other but, following a sensible arrangement, traffic was concentrated on the GWR site, which led to the LSWR terminus being used for goods traffic. (Lens of Sutton)

CHARD JUNCTION on the LSWR Salisbury to Exeter line with a GWR 2–6–2 tank at the head of the branch train to Taunton. (Lens of Sutton)

SECTION SEVEN

Somerset and Dorset

AS A FINAL LOOK at the railways of Somerset and Avon we move to the erstwhile Somerset and Dorset system, a much loved and still lamented route, which saw its last trains in 1966. This view is of Wincanton station, looking towards Cole, and shows the open side footbridge so different from the standard GWR design. Due to the track layout the platforms were slightly staggered, that on the right containing the main station buildings.

NEXT STATION NORTH WAS AT COLE, seen here looking back towards Wincanton. For some reason no canopy was provided for the main buildings while passenger access between the platforms was via a board crossing. The small goods yard was opposite the signal box and the station nameboard proclaimed 'Cole for Bruton' – a reference to competition with Bruton station on the GWR line from Frome.

AT EVERCREECH JUNCTION the main S & D route to Bath diverged from the branches to Highbridge and Bridgwater and, as at Templecombe, there was a thriving railway community. The photograph is looking north past the tall signal box, the engine and water crane obstructing a glimpse of the central siding laid beyond the footbridge.

AN EARLY VIEW OF SHEPTON MALLET (S & D) STATION, showing the main buildings which were located on the 'Up' side. Notice the wind-break at only one end of the building, which implies this was a draughty location at which to wait for a train. In later years the location was known as Shepton Mallet (Charlton Road) station.

ANOTHER VERY EARLY VIEW of the S & D line showing Windsor Hill tunnel prior to the line being doubled at this point. The original timber signal box is also visible, as is the line into Windsor Hill quarry.

DOUBLING OF THIS SECTION OF THE LINE was undertaken around the turn of the century and this photograph of Windsor Hill dates from around that time. It would appear excavations have just commenced. The quarry line is also visible to the left.

THIS VIEW OF MIDSOMER NORTON STATION looking south towards Evercreech was taken around 1900. The rural nature of the area is apparent from the roadway on the extreme left, while the unusual design of the station canopy is also to be noted.

SEEN FROM THE OPPOSITE END the basic nature of the facilities is apparent and what appears to be a greenhouse adjoins the platform. In later years Midsomer Norton regularly won an award in the 'Best Kept Station' competition due to the prize-winning blooms displayed on the platform.

A FINAL VIEW OF THE STATION looking towards Evercreech. The signal box here was of timber on a masonary base and controlled the sections to Chilcompton and Radstock. A block switch allowed it to be switched out of circuit when required.

TYNING'S BRIDGE AT RADSTOCK where the Somerset & Dorset line passed underneath the line to Tyning Colliery. To the left of the main girders can be seen a small arch which connected the headshunt from Ludlows Colliery and the British Wagon Co. Works siding to the main shunting yard. Notice also the tall signal box visible on the opposite side of the bridge.

SEEN FROM THE OPPOSITE SIDE the stone retaining wall, signal box and archway are again visible. The view looks south towards Writhlington, with the wagons standing on what is the 'Up' line.

JUST SOUTH OF MIDFORD STATION was an eight-arch viaduct which was widened in the latter part of the nineteenth century. At a number of locations on the viaduct timber formwork has been erected to support the new arches. In addition there appears to be a hoist and some scaffold at the site of the actual work.

BLASTING WORK IN PROGRESS during the opening out of a cutting near Tucking Mill viaduct. The precarious position of some of the workmen and the evident lack of any obvious safety equipment are apparent. This work was carried out during the period 1892–4.

WIDENING WORK AT TUCKING MILL VIADUCT in the early 1890s. The photographs on the following four pages show the top of the original single track structure as well as the lowering of equipment into position ready for the widening work to commence. The contractor's light railway is visible as are the new piers of the widened structure. A number of bowler-hatted gentlemen appear in the views, who were obviously the foremen, although one in particular would appear to have been senior to the rest and possibly the engineer in charge.

INSPECTING THE WORK at Tucking Mill Viaduct with the access trackwork used by the contractor seen through the arch. Despite the amount of additional work required for the widening, trains continued to run.

CONTRACTOR'S EQUIPMENT AND TRESTLING at Tucking Mill Viaduct, with a vertical-boiler steam engine visible.

THE BRANCH FROM EVERCREECH JUNCTION west towards Burnham and Bridgwater was flooded at Glastonbury in February 1897. The land here is very flat and only just above sea level, and consequently torrential rain could have a devastating effect. The shallow railway embankment shows above the water level, and a boy attempts some very basic fishing!

GLASTONBURY STATION with flood water all around. The extent of the difficulty is only too apparent in this photograph.

MANUAL LABOUR at the goods yard at Glastonbury with a hand crane being used to unload what appears to be sacking from a railway wagon. The heavy utilization of labour on the railway at this period in history is obvious with no less than five men present.

EXPERIMENTAL JARRANDALE SLEEPER at Glastonbury showing signs of severe deterioration after just two years.

EXTERIOR AND INTERIOR VIEWS of the signal box at Edington, the junction of the Burnham and Bridgwater branches.

THE STATION AT EDINGTON with the junction signals visible in the distance. In the background a branch train for Bridgewater can be seen waiting. The passengers on the platform are probably waiting for a Burnham service.

FLOOD WATER NEAR EDINGTON over ninety years ago, probably photographed at the same time as the floods affecting Glastonbury.

RAILWAY AND DOCK INTERCHANGE at Highbridge in 1897. The Somerset and Dorset Railway managed a not inconsiderable amount of traffic from the docks which included livestock and timber traffic. At the time the docks were also used by shipping from a number of foreign lands.

RAIL AND SEA INTERCHANGE at Highbridge Docks.

AT WELLS the Somerset and Dorset joined the GWR branch from Witham, which involved some interesting track formations. One of these is shown here – a 90° crossing within the Wells goods yard.

TO CONCLUDE THIS GLIMPSE of the former Somerset & Dorset system I could not resist the inclusion of two more views of civil engineering features of the line. The first, at Fiddleford Bridge, shows the bridge and a bearded inspector, while the view of Lyddon Bridge indicates where a serious brickwork failure has occurred. Unfortunately the S & D was a victim of the rationalization of the rail network in the 1960s with first its through services transferred away before finally closing in 1966. From a main line route, then, to nothing, it is still a railway the loss of which is lamented by many.